W9-BSV-342

Bicycles

Quinn M. Arnold

CREATIVE EDUCATION • CREATIVE PAPERBACKS

Published by Creative Education and Creative Paperbacks
P.O. Box 227, Mankato, Minnesota 56002
Creative Education and Creative Paperbacks
are imprints of The Creative Company
www.thecreativecompany.us

Design by Ellen Huber; production by Mary Herrmann
Art direction by Rita Marshall
Printed in the United States of America

Photographs by Alamy (Ivan Ekushenko), BigStock
(monkeybusinessimages), Getty Images (GibsonPictures, Ezra
Shaw), iStockphoto (monkeybusinessimages), Shutterstock
(artoflogic, Nor Gal, gorillaimages, Anton Gvozdikov, Inc, kenkuza,
Pavel Kobysh, LeManna, maxpro, Dudarev Mikhail, nito, Erica
Catarina Pontes, pattara puttiwong, resilva, Ljupco Smokovski,
Vladyslav Starozhylov, stockphoto-graf, Ivonne Wierink)

Copyright © 2020 Creative Education, Creative Paperbacks
International copyright reserved in all countries. No part of
this book may be reproduced in any form without written
permission from the publisher.

Library of Congress Cataloging-in-Publication Data
Names: Arnold, Quinn M., author.
Title: Bicycles / Quinn M. Arnold.
Series: Seedlings.
Includes bibliographical references and index.
Summary: A kindergarten-level introduction to the self-
propelled vehicles known as bicycles, covering their purpose,
parts, and operation, and such defining features as their wheels
and handlebars.
Identifiers: LCCN 2018053207 / ISBN 978-1-64026-168-6
(hardcover) / ISBN 978-1-62832-731-1 (pbk) /
ISBN 978-1-64000-286-9 (eBook)

Subjects: LCSH: Bicycles—Juvenile literature.
Classification: LCC TL412.A76 2019 / DDC 629.227/2—dc23

CCSS: RI.K.1, 2, 3, 4, 5, 6, 7; RI.1.1, 2, 3, 4, 5, 6, 7;
RF.K.1, 3; RF.1.1

First Edition HC 9 8 7 6 5 4 3 2 1
First Edition PBK 9 8 7 6 5 4 3 2 1

TABLE OF CONTENTS

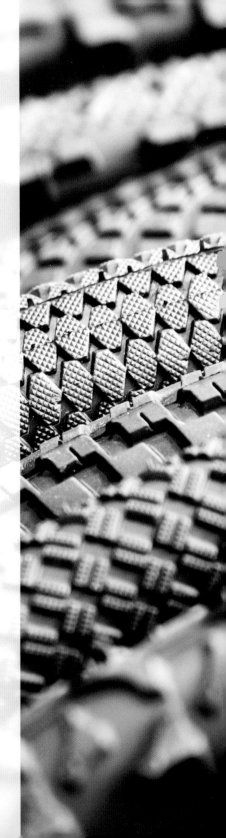

Time to go!

Bicycles are used outside. They can go on roads or trails.

The frame is the main part of the bike.

frame

The handlebars control the front wheel. They **steer** the bike.

Bike tires are made from rubber. Road bikes have thin tires. Mountain bike tires are wider.

Fat-tire bikes are used in the winter.

The rider pushes the pedals. This makes the wheels turn.

The brakes squeeze the wheel rims to stop the bike.

People who ride bikes
are called cyclists. They
wear helmets.

They sit on the seat, or saddle.

Bicycles can go fast!
They fly down dirt
trails. They race
on roads.

Go, bicycle, go!

Picture a Bicycle

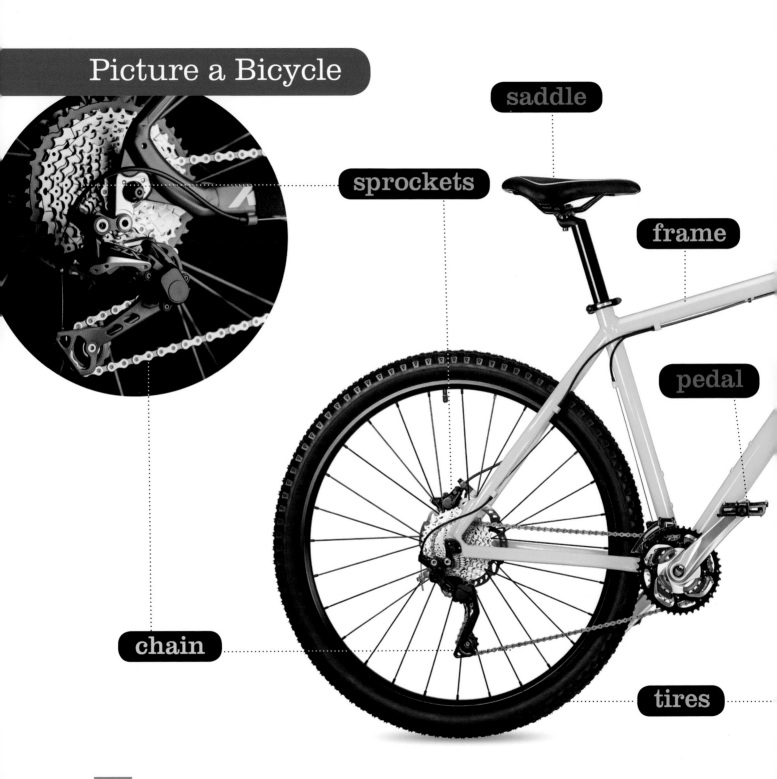

sprockets

saddle

frame

pedal

chain

tires

handlebar

brake lever

brake

spokes

rubber: a tough, durable material

steer: to turn or guide the movement of a vehicle

trails: beaten paths through rough country areas

Read More

Heos, Bridget. *Be Safe on Your Bike.*
North Mankato, Minn.: Amicus, 2015.

MacDumont, Sean. *Bikes Go!*
New York: Gareth Stevens, 2018.

Websites

Get Coloring Pages: Bike Coloring Page
http://www.getcoloringpages.com/bike-coloring-page
Print out pictures of bicycles to color.

NHTSA: Bicycle Safety Activity Kit
https://one.nhtsa.gov/people/injury/pedbimot/bike
/bskitboth/3152bskit/index.htm
Learn how to stay safe while bicycling!

Note: Every effort has been made to ensure that the websites listed above are suitable for children, that they have educational value, and that they contain no inappropriate material. However, because of the nature of the Internet, it is impossible to guarantee that these sites will remain active indefinitely or that their contents will not be altered.

Index